D1602281

Freedom Readers

SOLID GROUND

WritersCorps

Edited by Judith Tannenbaum
Foreword by ZZ Packer

Aunt Lute Books, San Francisco

Aunt Lute Books
P.O. Box 410687
San Francisco, CA 94141
www.auntlute.com

Executive Director: Joan Pinkvoss
Artistic Director: Shay Brawn
Managing Editor: Gina Gemello
Marketing Director: Marielle Gomez
Marketing Assistant: Chrissy Anderson-Zavala
Production: Chelsea Adewunmi, Andrea de Brito, Shahara Godfrey, Sarah Leavitt, Emily Ryan, Mona Lisa Safai

Cover and Text Design: Design Action Collective

This book was made possible through the support of Cultural Equity Grants, a program of the San Francisco Arts Commission; the Department of Children, Youth, and Their Families; the Department of Juvenile Probation; the LEF Foundation; the National Endowment for the Arts; the Northern California Independent Booksellers Association; the San Francisco Foundation; the Youth Arts Fund; the Vessel Foundation; the Zellerbach Family Fund; and individual donors.

Library of Congress Cataloging-in-Publication Data

Solid ground / WritersCorps ; Judith Tannenbaum, editor ; foreword by
ZZ Packer.
    p. cm.
    ISBN-13: 978-1-879960-71-8 (pbk. : alk. paper)
    ISBN-10: 1-879960-71-0 (pbk. : alk. paper)
    1. Youths' writings, American—California—San Francisco.
  2. American poetry—California—San Francisco. 3. American poetry
—20th century. 4. American poetry—21st century. 5. Youth—Poetry.
I, Tannenbaum, Judith. II. WritersCorps.
PS508.Y68S63 2006
811'.608092830979461—dc22
                2005037424

First Edition
Printed in the United States of America on recycled paper (50% post-consumer)
10 9 8 7 6 5 4 3 2 1

Acknowledgments

WritersCorps thanks editor Judith Tannenbaum for her many years of valuable service to our program. Judith is a gifted teacher, committed activist, and accomplished writer, and we are fortunate that she edited this collection.

Solid Ground exists because of thousands of San Francisco youth who have participated in WritersCorps classes and because of the talented writer-teachers who inspired them:

1994-2006 WritersCorps Teachers
Chrissy Anderson-Zavala, Cathy Arellano, Ellis Avery, Alegría Barclay, Stephen Beachy, Cherie Bombadier, Godhuli Bose, Tom Centolella, Carrie Chang, Elizabeth Chavez, Justin Chin, Eric Chow, Jorge Cortinas, Leslie Davis, Colette DeDonato, Victor Diaz, Aja Duncan, Rebekah Eisenberg, Mahru Elahi, Ananda Esteva, Kathy Evans, Sauda Garrett, Russell Gonzaga, Toussaint Haki, Susanna Hall, Lenore Harris, Donna Ho, Le Hubbard, Uchechi Kalu, Carrie Kartman, Melissa Klein, Jaime Lujan, Margot Lynn, Michelle Matz, Scott Meltsner, Elizabeth Meyer, Doug S. Miller, Maiana Minahal, Peter Money, Dani Montgomery, Kim Nelson, Hoa Nguyen, Sharon O'Brien, Beto Palomar, Steve Parks, Andrew Pearson, Elissa Perry, marcos ramírez, Christina Ramos, Victoria Rosales, Yiskah Rosenfeld, Jime Salcedo-Malo, Andrew P. Saito, Johnna Schmidt, Margaret Schulze, Alison Seevak, Chris Sindt, giovanni singleton, Chad Sweeney, Luis Syquia, JoNelle Toriseva, Elsie Washington, Chris West, Marvin White, Canon Wing, Will Wylie, Gloria Yamato, and Tara Youngblood.

We'd like to take this opportunity to recognize the dedicated staffs at the dozens of sites where WritersCorps teachers have taught.

We give thanks for our partnerships and collaborations, and are grateful to so many who work on behalf of young people in classrooms, neighborhoods, libraries, and programs throughout the City:

1994-2006 WritersCorps Sites
Balboa High School, Bay High School, Brava/DramaDIVAS, Career Resources Development Center, Center for Young Women's Development, Central City Hospitality House, Chinatown Youth Center, Chinese Progressive Association, Ella Hill Hutch Community Day School, Everett Middle School, Florence Crittenton House, Galileo High School, Gilman Playground, Girls After School Academy, Guerrero House, Huckleberry House, Ida B. Wells High School, Instituto Familiar de la Raza, International Studies Academy, Jamestown Community Center, Jovenes Unidos, Lakeshore Alternative Elementary School, Latinas in Theatre, Log Cabin Ranch, LYRIC, McAteer High School, Mercy Services California, Mission Girls, Mission High School, Newcomer High School, Office of Samoan Affairs, Phoenix High School, Project ACE/Wajumbe, Recreational Center for the Handicapped, San Francisco Community School, San Francisco Educational Services, San Francisco Public Library, Sisters4Life, SOMARTS/ArtSpan, Tenderloin AfterSchool Program, Tenderloin Reflection and Education Center, Visitation Valley Middle School/Viz Kids, Vietnamese Youth Development Center, Woodside Learning Center, Youth Drug and Treatment Center, Youth for Service, and Youth Guidance Center.

Special thanks to Joan Pinkvoss, Gina Gemello, and all the Aunt Lute staff for working with WritersCorps on another project, and for all the support they give to emerging writers.

A final thanks to the San Francisco Arts Commission for its commitment to WritersCorps and to the future of literary arts for all.

SOLID
GROUND

Table of Contents

3. Stress

4. Upheaval

5. Shock

6. After

Introduction

Upheaval, violence, chasm, and *split.* Such words describe San Francisco's Great Earthquake of 1906, and other temblors on the San Andreas Fault where the Pacific and North American Plates slide and grind. *Stress, displacement, turbulence, rupture:* words that also describe the lives of many contemporary youth who live along the metaphoric faultlines of immigration, economic inequity, turf wars, broken hearts, and the gunning down of young friends.

In commemoration of the 1906 earthquake, we have gathered 133 poems written by WritersCorps youth over the past twelve years. Since 1994, WritersCorps teachers have met with thousands of youth in public schools, detention centers, halfway houses, after-school programs, and many other community settings. Our teachers offer encouragement and skills to young people writing about their lives, visions, hopes, and fears. For many young poets, the act of writing itself comes to provide solid ground on which they can rest and from which they can speak.

"Hear the voice of the bard" William Blake proclaims in his late eighteenth century *Songs of Innocence and Experience.* One task of the poet has always been to tell the culture's story, to assert its identity, and to warn of the future. The poets in *Solid Ground* describe the stresses that affect their lives, and the tension that results. They render the strength and compassion born from their efforts to stay steady as the ground beneath them shakes. Each poet speaks for him or herself; each voice is unique. And also each voice adds to poetry's voice. The poems, taken together, tell a larger story—a bard's story, a griot's. A story of our times. These young writers have much to say about their individual experience, and about the world we all share.

Solid Ground opens with poems that praise the beauty of this world—the earth we walk on and the cities we live in. These poems express the wonder and joy of being alive. But beauty is not all our young people encounter. They also witness drama, drugs, homophobia, people without homes, dislocation, hatred, and violence. The stress builds, and the tension must be released. These inevitable earthquakes are followed by aftershocks, and then by a renewed passion to live a full life, even if the soil underfoot is shaky, even if "solid ground" is only fleeting.

So much is required of youth today. They are expected to grow into healthy human beings and productive citizens, often without being given requisite support and respect from family, from schools, or society. In order to better our children's lives, we must first listen to what they have to say—to themselves, to each other, and to parents, teachers, police, and presidents. The commitment of these young poets to write honestly and deeply demands of them accurate observation, as well as strong hearts. These same qualities are required of those of us reading their poems. WritersCorps is proud to provide this opportunity for you to hear from, and respond to, these courageous young poets. We invite you to their words in these pages.

Judith Tannenbaum

Foreword

Ten years ago, I was a public high school teacher who went home every night with sheaves of essays, homework and tests to grade. Grading was my least favorite teacher activity—I'd much rather answer a student face to face, scan a classroom to read the general mood of the class, or engage in class discussion than grade the standard (and often uninspired) five-paragraph essay on a book plucked from the school's decades-old (and often uninspired) reading list.

All that changed when our school devised a schedule that allowed for more electives. Suddenly, we were able to offer creative writing classes in addition to the standard English lit courses, and I had the honor of teaching—and grading—the school's budding poets, playwrights and future novelists. I began to look forward to grading. Students who were shy in class wrote as if they were singing from the mountaintops, and the "tough kids" revealed code, showed their vulnerability, told of lives lived motherless, fatherless; hopeless and rudderless.

In a world that cared little for what my students felt, hoped for, or believed in, writing often became their only salvation. I used to believe that only avid readers became writers, but after teaching creative writing, I witnessed a miracle: lackluster students of literature came away genuine readers when given a chance to express their own thoughts. Once their own proclivities were acknowledged and nourished, these students (many of whom used to groan about having to read a single page—not to mention a whole book) suddenly awakened, like newborn babes, ready to engulf the world of literature. They had learned that a well-crafted sentence or an apt line of verse could capture the timbre of their own heart-beats, and now these young lovers yearned for a connection to others like them. And so they read. And kept on reading. And kept on writing.

Though my years as a public school teacher are behind me, reading *Solid Ground* brought back that same feeling of awe that first night of reading my students' work. Who are these WritersCorps poets—thirteen and sixteen and eighteen—who speak with the wisdom of sages, yet the wonder and innocence of children? Who are these writers, who have somehow tapped at the raw feeling of what it means to be the immigrant kid who studies English into the late hours, hoping to put away the taunts from his classmates with his newfound fluency? Or what it means to see a friend gunned down outside your window? Or to see your father leave nothing behind but his keys?

Hurt, pain, longing and loss are hardly new signposts on the landscape of adolescence, so what makes these young writers so special? The poets contributing to *Solid Ground* do what writers do best: they make the general particular, and then, like magic, they turn around and make a specific experience universal. They transform bewilderment into rumination, chaos into resolve. These poems serve as talismans, as reportage, as reminders that we are all aswim, that we are all searching for solid ground.

ZZ Packer

Bedrock 1
the earth is an alphabet

Elements

Earth is the feeling of green
soft grass in the spring,
the touch of a bird's
light-brown feather.

Fire makes you want to burn
your fingers
black as burnt apple. It's the liquid
of a jeweler melting
a bar of shiny gold,
the fever of a dangerous
beast of the jungle.

Rain is the eye
of the wind blowing,
the sound of tsunami
in the clear ocean,
sound of a whispering friend.

Lily Nguyen, 11

The Earth's Poetry

Each wind of the earth
is her language,
and with that she makes sculptures
of beautiful forms.

The earth is an alphabet,
all the most beautiful words
are inspired by the earth.

The earth expresses her feelings
through her paintings:
all the mountains,
the seas
and forests,
all her colors
are the expressions of the earth.

She tells us this way,
with the beauty of nature,
helps us to write our own feelings,
like she does.

Sayra Colin, 14

The Letter O

open your mouth
say "ohooo"
the glasses
the moon
in the mid-autumn day

Wen Sheng Huang, 17

Everything Is Alive

The eyes of the house.
The belly of the ball pops out.
The tulips open their eyes.

The skin of the drum.
The building's leg was broken.
Winter held us in its snow.

The sweet voice of the wind.
The deep moan of the cave.
I was cradled by the arms of the house.

The river grabbed the boat with its hands.
The laughter of the cold
was all we could hear.

Joseph Crowell, 7

There

Why can't I be there
      sundried
amongst the mountain's
      clean air with
nappy hair and
      couldn't care.

To see my skin the deep
brown red of the dirt

for my feet to callus
but soften to the heart
beat of the earth.

Listen listen to the
space dance with my soul

I feel the love and I trust
what I don't want to know

I can't let go

Oh I feel so goodly

I feel so free
I wish everyone
who looks could
feel like me

Oh I wish you could see
the melodic colors make
love in the sky
Listen with your eyes

the awakening sun's cries

Loud orange and red
        tie dyes

watching the melting
of the night go by

feel the passion
the love is hot

in my favorite space
my welcomed spot.

Jamelvin W., 17

Everything I Dream

Leaves taste the springtime
falling from the tops of trees.
Everything I dream   becomes.

Ignacio Sanchez, 18

What Makes Me

The color of my life is the smoldering wood
of a campfire, the shadows of people taller than me.
The color of my life is a volcano erupting
against a cloudy sky, the burning coal
on my father's grill,
the blood that runs through my body.
The color of my life is the milk
in my sister's favorite cereal bowl,
a hawk soaring through the open skies,
and the soft, warm feeling
of my mother's arms around me
healing and protecting me from the pain.
It is a storm sneaking up
on a beautiful, sunny beach—the rivers that run
through the forests and mountains
and through the moods on my face.

The color of my life is the cotton
on my pillow where I lay my head
and dream the dreams of life.
The color of my life is the red, white, and pink
roses in my mother's unique garden.
It is the joy my father gives to me
with his strong, yet calm smile.
The color of my life lives in the voices
of people saying *do you care, don't hurt me, hello*
and other things like that.
The color of my life is the fear in me
trying to get out.
The color of my life is what makes me.

Genesis Flota, 14

Himalaya

I am the green of your eyes
and the red tiny tomatoes
filled with the water of sadness.

I am the snow bear
skating on a frozen lake
and the Himalaya
shrinking day after day
and everyone knows why.

It's hard to say my name.
That's why people call me my nickname, Abdul.

I am the soccer ball who never
betrayed its team and offered them
the World Cup.

I am a young male red apple
feeding humanity,
an African of Moroccan blood,
fishing for the fourth language.

I am a giant cactus all alone
in the center of the ocean
protecting myself from the noise.

I am the end of the week
at school, the day of my favorite food,
couscous on the moon.

I am the blood of the Red Sea,
calm and warm.

I am glad I was born.
If I wasn't, I wouldn't see
this wonderful life I am having now.

Abdessalam Mansori, 15

City Life

I feel myself
awakening finally
in the fragrant cherry blossoms,
in light bouncing from the blood-red
tiles of roofs.

I feel myself dying in the
city horizon,
lead paint peeling,
jet streak,
death bells chiming.

The alphabet of the city
is a water tower,
life
the color of a footstep. My dreams
are crowded
with ivory light and clouds.

City life is a
rose
growing in the crack
of a broken sidewalk.

Elizabeth Thompson, 13

Ghetto Girl

She rockin' the fresh braids with beads at the end
Reputation known for being bad, her and her friends
Lil' mama but her voice carry like yards
Known for gettin' vicious if you pull the wrong cards
She glistenin' and gleamin' with the gloss on her lips
She just love the attention so she put on a show
Don't mistake her for a dummy cuz she's smarter than
    you know
Disrespect is not an option cuz she wish you would
Don't get on her bad side cuz she will get 'hood
Ghetto girl rockin' the Baby Phat jeans
Lookin' and starin' with the mug oh so mean
She may seem rough but she does have a heart
She sings her butt off, it's her form of art
So quick to compare one thing to another
And don't put up a challenge cuz she will tell her brother
Ghetto girl rockin' the Jordan tennis shoes
So quick to judge them other fools
Can't nobody tell her nothin' cuz she know the street
She can handle her own battles and stand on her own
    feet
Some stand 5'5"
Seventeen years old with curls
They have all been tagged with the label
Ghetto girl

Deandra Kittles, 17

Views of San Francisco

I see buildings
people come in and out of every day,

murals of life that give
the earth its colors,

a trash can
where a lost cat sleeps.

The skies are gray
like an old man
after a stressful lifetime.

In the day streetlights sleep
and at night they come on.
They do this because they are nocturnal.

The streets
are patiently waiting
for someone
to cross them.

The buildings stand
and their legs are tired
but they can't sit down.
The parks are anxiously waiting
for kids to get out of school.

The cars go back and forth, not
caring where they go
as long as they are fed
with gas.

Johnny Herrera, 13

City Lust

City lust runs through my blood.
It's better than living in the country
watching mud.

In the city the air thick full of love
full of robbery licks.

In the city cars are fast.
Sometimes people in the city don't live to last.
City lust is like hopping a bus,
city lust is like tagging on a truck.

I love the city, the country I pity.

The biggest temptation is the city.
Nothing is as pretty as the night of the city.
Concrete planets are the districts, and the streets are
    the stars.
San Francisco beats Oakland by far.
City lust is like the back of the bus
cannot see in front but still have trust.

Craig F., 17

The Fall That Decorates the Streets

I am the red of the fire,
the color of blood,
and the enchilada's delicious flavor,
the white horse
   running in the prairie,
     and the white snow
       that lives in my soul.

I am the church
   where people vent their grief,
and the ocean where many animals live.

I am the jockey who runs like the wind,
and the jello
   that many people like.

I am Mexican.

I am the fall that decorates the street
   with the leaves from the trees.

I am the flower of the field
   that feeds the bees.

I am Saturday,
   the day in which families gather,
and the lake where people go fishing
   happy when the people visit.

Maria Marin, 15

What I Remember

What I remember about that day
is a group of boys around seven years old
practicing soccer at the park
with so much excitement
running from one place to another
kicking the ball the hardest they could.
Dogs running to get the ball.
Nice warm weather.

And me

looking up at the sky
trying to figure out if the clouds were really moving
trying to get a cookie from a little boy
happy to know I wasn't alone in this world
knowing it's not impossible to be happy.

Nothing about school problems
Nothing about my house

Mayra Flores, 13

In My Past Life...

I
was an elephant
running across the
plains of the desert
my feet pounded out
the hot beat
under the dry sun
In my past life
I was water
I came up from the ground in trickles
and rushed over
its parched surface
the zebras drank me
and gazelles
passed through me
In my past life
I was the sand
at the feet of the pyramids
I stuck to the toes
of the men who dragged
heavy rock over my back

In my past life
I was a beetle
and women picked me up
and put me into their pockets for
good luck
In my past life
I was a sound
I was the whisper of the mother
who put her child to sleep hungry
In my past life
I was the child
that watched my mother cry
because this was not the life she chose
But in her next life she will be the gazelle and I
   will be the grass
and I will feed her and she will run free
away from the cold cement walls who know her
   too well.

Gabby Cole, 17

She's Awake

And when you wake up
Your head is waiting
For the night to come again.
She's awake, cover
Her head and wait
For the day to end
And the night to
Begin for a dream.

Nalashi Almendral, 9

Between Earth and Sky

The sun shines around the sky
The world spins in space
The mermaid sings while swimming in the ocean
The crown goes on top of the king's head
The umbrella keeps you safe from the rain
The rose smells like beautiful perfume that makes you
   fall in love

Diana Marenco, 10

Faultline 2
what happened to this world?

Broken Glass

in the street
in the sand
in the dirt

don't someone care
if the kids get hurt?

Marco Moon, 17

What Happened?

What happened to the happiness and joy?
They changed into badness and selfishness.
What happened to the sharing and caring?
They changed into stealing and hating.
What happened to the homemade good meals?
It changed into fast food.
What happened to taking care
of each other for their health?
It changed into killing each other for wealth.
What happened to the cleanness of the world?
It changed into the dirtiness of the world.
What happened to world peace?
It changed into war.
What happened to this world?
Hate, cheating, lying, stealing, fast food, war,
bombs, dirt, violence, abuse, drugs,
gangs, suicide, killing, shooting.
What happened
to this
world?

Lilian Dominguez, 12

Being a Kid Is Hard

Being a kid is hard,
like dueling a giant in the courtyard.

Being a kid is about surviving school,
acting cool, trying to follow every rule,
escaping from the crazy teacher Ms. Bull,
running from John who looks like a mule,
trying not to act like the complete fool.

Being a kid is hard,
like dueling a giant in the courtyard.

Being a kid is about playing around,
putting your music to a real high sound,
going on a roller coaster round and round,
getting a million rebounds,
trying to stop being earthbound,
to escape the government
and join the underground
where you can't be found
and trying to avoid the
neighbor's bloodhound.

Being a kid is hard,
like dueling a giant in the courtyard.

Being a kid is about being slim,
passing gym, telling the entire class
the meaning of homonym, synonym, antonym.
It is about trying not to look grim,
getting a good trim, when you can take a swim,
and best of all, hanging out with your homie Tim.

Being a kid is hard,
like dueling a giant in the courtyard.

Sebástian Hernández, 10

Drama

There is too much drama in my school.
Kids are always spreading rumors
and getting into fights.

There is too much drama in my church.
Some people call themselves Christians,
they truly ain't.

There is too much drama in my classroom.
Students are always talking back to the teachers.

There is too much drama on Mission Street.
People are always selling drugs or
jacking old ladies' purses on the bus.

There is just too much drama in this world.
Nobody knows how to live peacefully.

Bianca Sanchez, 12

Friends in Temptation

Best friends all our lives.
Not him not her just us.
Not just you not just me but we.
It's hard to be friends in the drama
because of the temptation in the world.
Like boys and girls, drugs, sex, weapons
and fightin' instead of writin'.
When you get into temptation
your friends lose a friend
because you couldn't resist
that lustful kiss of temptation.
Sometimes it's hard
but you have to fight
just like you fought
that girl pushing
and punching
kickin and scratchin
pullin out hair.
You can fight your friends
but oh no you wouldn't
dare fight
temptation.

Takeyah Chandler, 14

Ain't Nobody Wanna Be Gay

"Ain't nobody wanna be gay"
The wisest wisdom
From a girl my age
"Ain't nobody wanna be gay"
Ain't nobody wanna be themselves
In a place that won't let you be
Ain't everybody wanna be a somebody
Portrayed on the TV
Ain't everybody wanna be immortalized
As a nameless stereotype
There ain't nobody that's gonna stray
From the dogmatic radio hype
Ain't nobody wanna be lost
Ain't nobody wanna be confused
Ain't nobody wanna be alone
Ain't nobody gonna be excused
Ain't nobody wanna be themselves
Ain't nobody wanna be free
Ain't nobody wanna know nobody
Who ever tried "to be."

Celia La Luz, 17

Where I Live

Where I live
the crack heads roam
and the hookers moan
and liquor washes away their pain.

Where I live
trash blows with the breeze
and folks fall to their knees
and beg God for deliverance.

Where I live
you might get stabbed for a dollar
and you can hear the whiny mutts holler
about nothing and everything all at once.

Where I live
the yuppies pass by and frown
and the cops will beat you down
if you give them the slightest lip.

Where I live
I walk around on my feet
trying to find something to eat
and dream of living elsewhere.

Joey Martin, 17

The Bottles

The broken bottles embrace
ash and dust at night
and then come the humans
and call the police.

Joaquin Rinaldi-Petroni, 10

The Bus Driver

All these different kinds of people
boarding my car. These left and right
thorns twisting my mind. One second, a smell
of cologne. The next, the smell of rotting fish.

Voices everywhere calling my brain to explode.
Not one step to move all day
and that brake—that's what I worry about.
Here I am minding my own business,
and I have to drop my soul down
on that black pedal.

I may end up in court
getting sued by a person who flew
through the windshield.
Kids all ages with five-inch markers
sticking out of their pockets. I see them tagging
but talking to them or yelling at them
won't do no good. They'll never learn
doing that can land you in jail.

All I know is people
don't be giving me no respect.
Not thinking.
I take them where they wanna go
because I'm the bus driver.

Shahid Minapara, 13

A Big Change in My Life from China to America

America is gold
But I don't know
How to use it.
China is a desert
And I am sand.
The wind blows to another place.
America is a prairie
And I am grass.
China is a tree
And I am the leaf.
I drop to another place.
China is sky
And I am cloud.
China is cloud
And I am rain.

Wu Jia Yi, 18

The Burning Bush

Why do we vote red
when our intentions are blue?
If the votes were fixed
would you believe it's true?

Why does the president always stutter
when he's in a meeting?
If he were a puppet
could you see the strings from the ceiling?

Why does he gotta make jokes
when kids are dying?
If all he's selling is dreams
then I ain't buying.

Why does he want to have things
that can't be bought?
So if weapons were the reason
he's the only one who thought so.

Why does our leader
have such sinister intentions?
If not oil then...
what did he forget to mention?

Why be led by someone who
used & bought blow?
If the economy's so broke
tax the dealers who got dough.

John Williams, 16

Homeless Personification

About sixty pounds on top of
Sores and blisters
Oh, I wonder how it would feel
To own a pair of sandals
Rope cutting off my circulation
No water to wash my hands
Something other than a hat
To keep my head warm
Knits are woven to keep me visible
Some sort of battlefield surrounds me
Survival of the fittest
I feel like a potato in a sack
I am not a prop
You will not find proof of purchase
This is not a stage
Just take the picture and collect
Your earnings

Ynez Agurs, 18

Get Stereotyped

I have buried you.
I told you that many times.
However,
You keep yelling at me,
At my not standard American spoken-English.

You already know clearly
I am a new immigrant, staying in the U.S. for a short
    time—only a year.
English is not my first language,
I was not born here,
And I am an ELD student.

You may not know me too much.
When it is 11 PM
I still continue doing my homework though it is easy for
    you.
I keep practicing the standard American English.
I try to speak English fluently,
And I hope I can be a real American in five years, while
    you are laughing.
I feel uncomfortable, like a hopeless baby bird studying
    flying.
I feel so sad, cause although I work hard,
I won't be angry with you because I know I am a small
    immigrant.

Xue Sun, 18

Spaces

Outside splinters of light gather
where freeways buzz
Cars scrape concrete
chaos stitched to ends of city streets

Footsteps marble water puddles
remainders of hamburger wrappers
scattered like a half formed sentence
forgotten
cars overflow with junk
a jumble of memories upon memories

Mud cakes sides of my shoes
Above freeways buzz like an old man's anger
His voice like factory windows breaks

"This is my neighborhood, not yours," he says.

Annie Yu, 16

Invasion

You all need to stop invading
and stop parading.
This is our hood, our homes.
Can't you get that through your domes?
We only have one district
and this is it.
Can't you see that you don't fit?
What? You enjoy watching us go
cuz rent is too rich and we too poor.
Ya'll got money, go elsewhere.
This is what we can afford.
Ain't that fair?

Tell me something.
Does it put a smile on your face
to see the Mission invaded with fancy cafés?
Does it make you happy to see more of your kind?
Please, do tell me what goes on in those wicked lil' minds.
Let me guess, it's reach.
Nah, uh, it's got to be a goal
to see the beautiful people of the Mission go.

You know it kills me
to see my people struggle and strive,
to keep a roof over they heads
and food on the table to keep alive,
messed up homes with no heater.
What? Air conditioning?
Nah, we ain't got none of that either,
but we don't complain
cuz we can't afford more.
So let us keep our mouths shut
about broken windows or even a broken door.

You see the point that I am tryna make
is that you all took our homes before.
I guess ya'll got a habit
of taking what's not yours.
But I'm a tell you,
this is more than just a place to sleep.
It's something that goes way too deep,
something that you wouldn't understand,
being that you never could leave colored land.
So once again we are defeated.
But live with the guilt
that you used your color,
so you cheated.

Nez Carrasco, 18

Stairs

The backs of migrant workers
all ways bent down

Armando Aguilar, 14

I, Too, Sing America

I, too, sing America
I, too, hear gunshots each night
I, too, hear police sirens in my neighborhood
I, too, see candles, flowers and balloons on my block
   where people died
I, too, touch my family members that died on my block
I, too, smell McDonald's/Chinese food in Fillmoe
I, too, wish that they didn't shoot Ray Bass
I, too, like living in Fillmoe even though there's violence
   and drugs
I, too, wish that everyone can live and not die
I, too, am America

T.J. Williams, 13

Truth Hurts

Raised in a world with hate and violence.
Isolated in my room and wait in silence,
little scared child, parents are violent.
Teary eyes in abandoned space, and silent.
Didn't ask for life but that was given
in the back, in pitch black.
Not adapted to living, innocent infant
but yet still guilty.
Project Housing Living Conditions filthy.
Entrapped in this hell, asking who sent me,
stomach full from the food
but the heart is empty.

Diante J., 17

Life of a Toy Soldier

Created from the heat of melting plastic
Before his body was formed he was a stick
As the melting plastic cooked it formed a heart
Soon to be torn apart

All that's in his mind is war
No love, no passion, no emotion
Only a brutal warrior fighting for a cause no one
    understands
Always has to have caution

Drums start to play
As it gets close to the end of the day
Footsteps march
Into trenches

The pain of being material with no feeling
No pain even if you're falling
As the darkness approaches
Everyone is frightened even the cockroaches

The rain drops on his face
As he realizes it's time to go
He holds his gun on his shoulder
Walks away with a gaze
Never again will he let go of his weapons

War is a hateful thing
No such thing as a peaceful war
Only pain and suffering

Nay Win, 17

Fallen Rose Petals

Lord O Lord
Do you see what's going on
All our young black men will soon be gone
Mothers have to say good-bye to their sons
Men dying like flies, one by one
What is the point of young men having dreams
If they are not able to pursue them
It's not enough to know what's right
Unless we're wise enough to do it

Don't join the crowd to be acknowledged and accepted
Be yourself even if you're left out and rejected
Although you don't want to know the truth
You'll have to one day live it
It is also not enough to want to love
Unless you care enough to give it

Even though the rose petals are fallin'
It was time to go
For this one
God was callin'

Kenessa Robinson, 13

Life

The leaves are strewn
on my bed
like my hopes

Edgar Y., 19

Where Were You

for Dr. Martin Luther King, Jr.

Stay with that dream
That makes you want to ring
Freedom!

Cause I too have a dream that stands in this time
where you need more than a dime on these streets to
    survive.
I wish all of this would stop,
youth killing each other with them silver shells.

Dr. King, please tell me,
What would you do if you'd seen
the things I see today?
Your brothers, my brothers
are taking each others' lives.

Levantay crosses the street into a rain of bullets.
People duck and scream as the blood from
his chest forms an ocean of hate.

I need guidance.
I gotta call on those before me
who also had that dream
that continues to ring
Freedom!

As EMTs give CPR, news cameras
form a circle to capture images of Levantay
of the young lifeless body with their lenses
which take his soul and never return it.

Now follow me to this country, Iraq.
Look there. You see this man on his knees
with puffy eyes looking to the sky.
Now look around, there are weapons everywhere.
This country is being destroyed
and children are dying.
Please, Dr. King, I need guidance
in this world with so much violence.

Rosa Parks' boycott was hard
like the concrete Levantay stained.
How will I take up your voice, Rosa,
to turn to America and speak these words
and ask these questions?

Where were you when this boy fell?

Walkin on the beach with your dog?
Did you hear the gunshot that
put the hole in his chest and the stain
on the sidewalk?

I was in the shower,
but I saw the stain.

If you look at the bloodstain
you can still see his face.
It looks like the Girbaud tee
he was wearin.

If you lean close and look
beyond the footprints of the pedestrians
you can almost see his face expression
when the bullet hit him.

Examine the stain.
You can hear his last word
and almost smell his last breath.

Some people say they can see
the imprint of the design of his freshly parted braids.
Some say they can see the shoe print
of his brand new Jordans.

My question to you is,
where were you when this boy fell?

When this boy fell a grandma was
pulling fresh cookies out of an oven.

When this boy fell a man was
picking his three year old up from day care.

When this boy fell a mother was
giving birth to her new baby boy
and she named him Levantay.

Where were you?

Dr. King, was that your body fallen on the sidewalk?
Are you speaking through me now?

Marie Antoinette Osborne, 16

My 'Hood

I am talking about my 'hood now
If you listen I will tell you what I know.

You say you want to be a thug
On the corner slangin drugs.

Just because you got gat
It don't mean you got it like that.
> They say
> You live by the gun
> You die by the gun.
Well, right now it seems like
I'm living by the gun
Just a gunshot across the street.

Brothers dying
Mothers crying
Saying

Somebody help me!
My baby dying by the minute
Just because "so and so"
didn't get their money
on the day they wanted it.

So they go out there and
get smoked like a joint.

I'm ten years old and I already know.
Ain't it a shame?
But, hey, what can I say?
Life is life and that ain't going to change.

Angelica "Jelly" Pineda, 10

Stop the Useless Killings

some rappers use ghetto life as an excuse for their violent
   rhymes
sayin, it aint my fault i grew up in violent times
they rap about .44s, teck 9s, and street sweepin
i try to flow about succeedin
how to stay breathin

say they can only rap about what they know
ghetto life and death
i don't know about success so when i breathe
i'm wasting my breath
all this music about death
got kids thinking that killing is cool
buyin triggers ready and willing to pull
they wanna pump these killas full of lead
for a murder 2 weeks ago—2 weeks later at least 3 more
   dead
kill one then get killed by another who gets killed by
   another
the endless death cycle, they are murderous brothers

there is no good that comes from taking a life
except, some say, satisfaction from cappin the dude
that shot ya boy twice
but that feeling won't last too long
cuz the homeboyz of that kid you hit
now they want you gone

how can we stop these senseless acts
of mindless violence
death should be grieved but keep your vengeful
    thoughts
hidden in silence

STOP THE USELESS KILLINGS

Alex Trono, 17

My Life

My world is Medusa crazy, loud
unruly and unbearable.
In my world, if you die with your eyes open,
you deserve it.
In my world, nothing
no one
no where
no shelter can save you.
Oh, you think you hard?
You think you can stare down that barrel
with that bullet comin' at you?
No No No
You think you Superman,
huh? You untouchable? Boy, please.
Not when that gun comin'.
Your world is an amusement park.
Let's take a tour.
First ride you see rapers, beaters, and hoes.
You see people killing people
and people killing themselves.

In *my* world, it's damn crackin'
when you walk down the street.
Don't nobody mug
Nobody questions you
Nobody talk shit
Nobody kill
Everybody die with their eyes closed.
Oh you should see it,
It's beautiful.
You should taste it, *Freedom*
We never had that before.
But even with my eyes closed
I can't see it.
Damn, things got to change.

Katelyn Williams, 13

Free

You say we free
Then why you like a Siamese twin to one area
Can't go outside your boundaries 'cause
Brothas wanna bury ya
For reasons even uncertain to you
Young brothas dyin' so rapidly now
It's like damn we lost him too

And you say we free
Talkin' about you got freedom of speech
Stayin' in one part of town can't expand
Your brain, the sky
Seems impossible to reach
That hopeless feelin', thinkin' the only thing you can
Do right is sleep

And you say we free
Trapped in a concrete jungle
Where everybody wants to be a lion
Feelin' like there's no sense in climbin'
To the top because brothas on the streets
Are like crabs in a bucket
Always pulling you down

And you say we free
Then why we cheat our brains
It's hard to be creative with the cells that remain
Minds trapped in chains inside a cage
Screamin' for freedom
But blunt smoke and alcohol are the only things
You feed 'em
(Talkin' 'bout food for thought)

And you say we free
While you livin' on the edge waitin' to get pushed
Black on black crime is reachin' an all-time high
In the record books
It's hard to focus on the path ahead
When you always have to give your shoulder an
    overlook

And you say we free
Lack of self-motivation keep brothas
In altercation lack of destination
Leads to no demonstration
For our youth so we think entertainment
Is the only thing we can do

And if we free
Why we livin' with no sense of reality
Young brothas dyin' fast 'cause they want
Respect like your majesty

And you say we free
But in all actuality we still
Livin' in slavery minus the visual chains
Now society holds us captive with
Visuals to the brain it's a shame
How magazines make people do the insane
Dismantle their frame

And you tellin' me we free
Most people speak love but don't
Live love and love for each
Other will take the shackles off
Our feet

Now ask yourself
Are you
Free?

Eric Foster, 17

Stress 3
waiting for a storm to come

World

The earth is spinning
but nobody feels it.

The globe
is
getting
DIZZY!

Arianne Aman, 11

What Do You Do?

What do you do if
The sky falls down
On the earth?

What do you do when
The government closes
The school?

What do you do when
The ghosts attack
The earth?

What do you do when
The sky rains rockets?

What do you do when you
See the birds
Bleeding on the trees?

What do you do when
You hear about people
Fifty-five years old who haven't
Been in peace?

Bassam Esmail, 17

The Clock Is Ticking

I am waiting for a storm to come,
for it can take me
to somewhere
that a man has not been before.
I am waiting.
The clock is ticking,
so am I.
I am going upside down,
like a cat,
sucking catnip.

Teddy Williams, 10

A Poem

is like a burning city
with dirty streets,
people
sleeping in the sewers,
rats
vanishing into tunnels.

Like putting the earth's core
into words
and making the poem
hesitate.

The streets are burning in fear.
The buildings are lit up by flames.

A poem

is putting the burning city
into words.

A poem is my firing mind
lighting up
with magical thoughts.

Rosy Mena, 13

Superstitious

I once imagined a world within a world
a place where everything would be backwards and
   curled.
Picture blue trees fully bloomed only to shrink
to a smaller size, and taller guys swallow pride and
   don't blink.
Mirrors inside of mirrors to see self a thousand times
living life with repetitive dreams of dreams of seeing
   blind.
To wander with a sharp stride past vacant buildings
that join the trashy streets, under a dark skylight
lit dimly in the night.

Neil B., 17

I Am

I am the poet who cannot flow
The mute who speaks with a pen and paper
I am the opposite of wind
Seen but not heard
I am spoken but not said
A silent
Word

Alexander O. Muhammad, 16

Farewell

Thursday five o'clock.
Tension in the air.
Tension in the earth.
Melancholy on my aunties' faces
And tears from my grandma's eyes.
My little cousins run in the airport.
Their smiles spread gaiety in between sadness
As they beg me to take them with me
On what looks like another vacation.
They don't understand now it's good-bye
Without a further come back.

The sounds of the huge machine
Are a thunder in the sky.
The strong buzz of the turbine
Predicts the disaster
Under my feet.
When the plane takes off
My pathway breaks
In two pieces.
A tremendous earthquake beats through my life.
I find myself in two different places after boarding that
    plane.
I stand on the north side, in front of me a wide hole
That pulls me apart from my homeland.

Every night when I submerge in the darkness
The unique desire in my dreams
Is to cross the hole left by the quake
And walk once again in the place I was born.
Fifteen years of my life in flames and ruins.
And when I wake I must rise from the ashes
To build a new home
In the upper level of the American continent.

Jorge Aburto, 17

Closed Window

Sadness is a face with tears.
It is a waterfall that is flowing fast.
Sadness is a man and a woman breaking up.
It is a heart that is crying for love.
Sadness is a cut that is bleeding.
It is electricity that has no energy to control things.
Sadness is a cloud that is raining through the darkness.
It is a pipe that has nowhere to go.
Sadness is a window that is closed all the time.
It is a marker that is running out of ink.

Lovely Lopez, 10

Air

I climb to the top,
thinking I'm getting somewhere,
but all I get are more things
to worry about:
how to please you and the rest
of the world,
slowly losing everything I
ever loved
because you don't think
I deserve it.
Always giving me critical
feedback,
and when I don't want your
feedback, you give me more,
stepping on my throat,
taking all of my air.

Jermaine LeBrane, 14

Stored Dreams

A dream that doesn't come true gets stored
in an attic where the cobwebs are,
stays where I keep my clothes,
stays in the clouds, pours like rain,
flies with the wind,
stays in a balloon until it pops.

Holly Enrile, 13

A Question of Love

Love
How can love be a man abusing a woman and then
    telling her he is sorry?
Is love a dealer happily selling his drugs to the addicted?
How can love be breaking up a love affair cause one
    person is too skinny or too fat?
Is love lost when best friends get mad and stop speaking
    to each other?
How can you say you love and walk by homeless people
    sitting in the rain under the freeway?
Is love for your brothers going to funeral after funeral as
    the drive-by shootings continue
To go on and on?
How can love be countries killing women and children
    and soldiers for oil or religion?
Or is love just always being there, or is it a scare?
Or is love to care? Wait...think of it as a dare?

Ayinde Bell, 14

Who Will Break the Chain?

Since yo mom was on drugs
Yo father left her
Since he left her
He didn't know she was pregnant
Since he didn't know she was pregnant
She had you by herself
Since she had you by herself
You grew up without a father
Since you grew up without a father
You was raised by the streets
Since you was raised by the streets
You only knew fast money, sex and drugs
Since you only knew fast money, sex and drugs
You never did time on a job just time in jail
Since you did time in jail you hated the police
Since you hated the police you didn't follow the law
Since you hated the law you chilled with the lawbreakers
Since you chilled with the lawbreakers
There was never positive vibes
Yo mind stayed in the gutta
Since yo mind stayed in the gutta
You had weak conversation
You met weak girls
Since you met weak girls
They mind was just like yours
Since they mind was just like yours
Ya'll had nothing to offer your young
Since you had nothing to offer your young
They grow up just like you
Who will break the chain?

Eric Foster, 16

Can't See the Clouds

all this crime, lives at stake,
mothers at sixteen, doing lines to escape,
all these drive-by hits, dealers don't realize
they're selling people's suicide,
that's why I quit, murders, robberies,
kidnappings, kids
stabbin other kids,
blastin an' accidents happenin,
identities mistaken,
putting clips in his face an'
he ain't even the Jason you chasin',
poverty mixt with greed, 40s never
stop pouring, it's hard, we ain't rich
in our pockets, but we ain't poor in our hearts,
weed, heroin, shrooms and coke,
can't drown in misery cuz we're
doomed to float,
drugs wouldn't help,
witnesses getting stitches
for seein somethin they couldn't help,
some people get locked in
whether it's jail or projects,
we can never cut our losses,
struggle lost in whatever the cost
to bubble,

help us, oh ya'll turnin a deaf ear,
do you fear me? nah,
you despise my type, you
will hear me, and fear me,
you would be wise to, cuz unlike you
I'm goin' die truth,
and I got nothing to lose,
cuz statistics done by you,
show I'm gon die soon,
so now you scared,
you wanna be scared,
imagine getting paid minimum wage
till a gage sends you to your grave,
now imagine a place
where that happens every day,
get in a bad situation and you gotta get out,
get out? how? gotta rap yo way out,
show these marks some real jazz,
if only I could...
I just want my tears to come
swimming back up my chin and cheeks
to my eyes, so I'd have a clear view...
of the absent clouds.

Robin Black, 16

When It Rains

When it rains all our hearts get wet
And get lost in the sky, trying to find that light
That makes me keep going day by day
When it rains it looks like God is crying for all
Human faults, looks like angels cry around my face.
Puddles in the streets remind me of a big ocean trying
To find another way to move. When it rains all my
Affairs are going through the air, flying without destination
All my questions are missing.
Each drop became a hope, each hope became a life.
It's hard to think that our world is not
Complete yet, that we are not complete yet.
Rain is a drop going down, a hope going to nowhere.

Ingrid Z., 16

My True Name

I'm a screamin', shoutin', don't-know-what-to-do
today starts anew
stick my tongue out but hardly ever pout
kinda gyrl.

I'm a pray for rain
in emotional pain
a little insane
kinda gyrl.

I'm a hug-you-before-I-kill-you
never say never 'til you need to
cause I can say whatever the heck I want to
kinda gyrl.

I'm a basketball throwin'
my mind is always growin'
love it when the wind is blowin'
love to do-re-mi-fa-so-la-ti-do-in'
kinda gyrl.

But only you
call me by my secret name.

Baby blue
like the sky before
twilight.

Call me *cherry blossom*
like the ones in my dreams.

Call me *courage* and *mystery*.

I am the vacant lot across the street
with eyes that see the cityscape,

a blue rose just budding,

Madame Butterfly,
a teddy bear with one leg,
ice cream melting off the cone.

Call me unique, happy,
the high winds blowing away the trouble.

I am
the glacier
that sunk the Titanic.

Elizabeth Thompson, 13

Fwump Frump

Look me over with your monocle of air,
I dare you.
I cannot fathom why you simply look on,
commentless,
eyebrows raised,
golden jewelry sparkling.
Just say you hate it!
Just say I'm not good enough
because I don't belong to
the elderly ladies' country club.

Don't ride around the truth in a horse drawn carriage
or stretched limousine—you look down upon me.
I hate to disappoint you
but your money makes you nothing,
nothing but a frump.

What I would give to see you collapse.
The dust rises through the ground
as you fall down through the air.
You lay there as nothing but a big frump lump.

Fwump, my ears open to the peaceful end.
I'll be waiting to hear that sound so I can finally relax.

FWUMP

Grace Harpster, 13

Not Today

On my way to school
off to another day
so redundant they blend together
like the fog and the sky
A hue of gray
bathes us early commuters
some off to school
some off to work
but never off of routine
Melancholy blues
on the 24
My bus to monotonous

I cry into my notebook
as if it is my open hands
or my mother's bosom
Life has been robbed of its color
Life is like a black and white printer
unable to present the world
in anything but variations of black and gray
We are shadows of our creative selves
We are nine to fivers
We are Superman
when he is mild mannered

Some of us sit
some of us stand
as the bus struggles up the hills
I pray for the world to stop
My pent up anger
a sort of molten rock
brewing, glowing, in an array of colors and heat
pushing itself forward

This is not a regular day
I will not allow it

My notebook is now too heavy to carry
tears I shed when nothing is wrong
The bus makes its way down the hill
it worked so hard to get up
slowly releasing the brakes
Everyone shifts their weight
We are all on automatic pilot
We are all too blind to see it

I will no longer allow it
I get up screaming
A banshee yell
so loud it explodes
the Plexiglas windows
I once viewed the world pass me by
NO MORE!
Blood vibrant and alive
cuts down ears
clashing against the surrounding scenery
The bus driver hits the brakes
Everyone falls forward
except for me
I continue to scream
lava shooting from the cracks in the streets
from every orifice in my body
burning everything it touches
A geyser of frustration
gushing out my mouth
No
Not today
Today will not be a regular day

Antonio Caceres, 22

The Neutrals' Wake-Up Call

I am the "let be" in between bygones and bygones.
I am the battlefield
Iraqis and Americans die on.

Between the Batman and Joker
I am the Gotham.
I am the Fahrenheit 911
between Mr. Bush and Mr. Bin Laden.

Wake up, wake up, wake up.
Separate the lies from the truthful,
the vital, the unuseful,
and in all this I am the neutral.

I do not love Hate, nor hate Love,
I am not real nor made up,
blood, I am what arrives early
in the morning before the dump truck.

I am the neutral,
                    the call
to wake y'all
up.

Robin Black, 16

Our Year

This is the year that we rise to the occasion.
Our will is strong,
we gonna free this nation.

This year we're changing the rules, so you better watch
    out.
Through our struggles rose power,
we gonna do more than shout.

This year we stop prison guards in their tracks.
Grab the keys.
Unlock the shackles.
Take our loved ones back.

This is the year we're not settlin' for scraps.
We're takin' what's ours,
no questions asked.

This is the year they prayed would never come.
In defense they planted poison seeds of picket fences
and unattainable American dreams,
not once thinking that their master plan was weak at
    the seams.

But it was, and this year we're bustin' it open,
takin' back the land that they know is stolen.

This is the year our people will rise,
free our brothers and sisters without fear in our eyes.

Jessica Nowlan-Green, 21

Revolve

Revolver
Taking lives one bullet at a time
After a revolution of the chamber
It must begin again
Reload

Is this the revolution that we want?

Revolt
It must begin to change
After the evolution of danger
Taking control one day at a time
Revolution

Corey Largent, 17

Where the World Changes

Today I feel like a woman standing
On the mountain,
Like a hero getting ready to war from a country
Where the world changes.
I feel worried and sad,
Like sun and moon in a solar eclipse,
Afraid, not free, and uncomfortable.
I don't even know what to do.
I'm a baby getting ready to go from fetus to cradle
A child ready to walk.
A sun brighter than everything
So peaceful in the world.

Chau Thai, 16

Upheaval 4

glass hitting the floor

Recipe for Fire

A cup of flames.
Chile for spice.
A bucket of the sun
to keep it burning.
A sprinkle of pepper and salt.

Pour a teaspoon of lava.
A bucket of dragon fire-flame hot breath.
Add some blood
to lighten up the taste.
Add some red for the coloring.
Make it at night.

Saman Minapara, 8

even the cool wind
it also changes temper
screaming through the street

Xuan Luo, 16

Afraid of the Dark

They cuff me and take me
to a place where I don't want to go.
The car stops at a sudden stop.
All I hear is voices with a loud plump,
the gates open.
I feel like I'm blinded
cause where I'm at is dark.
Dark like pitch black.
Five hours later I'm still in this hole,
hole but a dark hole.
I'm hungry so I knock loud
to ask for food. No answer.
So I ask myself is this a dream?
My mistakes that I made
was similar like a scene.
I wake up and find myself
beggin' like a fiend.
Check back to reality
cause this is not a dream.

Cecil T., 17

What Is a Hurricane?

The hurricane is the groan of the gods,
the dancing of the air,
a giant housewife using her vacuum cleaner,
a shortcut straight to heaven,
a big whirlpool in the sky,
a robber doing his work,
ghosts running around a spot.

Chang Lin, 15

Think Twice

Someone has stolen my crown
stuck a knife in my heart
and turned me upside down.
Tied me to the ceiling
and now I'm eternally bleeding.
Rolled the dice
for my life
and didn't even
think twice.

Marlon R., 19

The Last Time

What I remember about that day:

My dad went away.
I was crying.
He left nothing behind but his keys.

His bed was empty that night.
The next morning
he didn't come back.

Miuler Carrillo, 12

Without Parents, Without Partners

Stand on the grassland
let the rain and wind lash your face
Alone is like an earthquake

Wen Sheng Huang, 17

Learning English Is Like

swimming in an ocean with many sharks
trying to see something when you are blind
walking on thorns without shoes
trying to hear something when you are deaf
staying in the sun without clothes for five hours
wanting to walk but not having legs
trying to type your schoolwork on a computer that
    doesn't have a keyboard
playing soccer without players
doing the English test without an explanation
going to the moon without a rocket
surviving somewhere that has no air
writing in a notebook that doesn't have pages
cutting paper without scissors
dancing without music
finding water in a desert
flying without wings
trying to see something in the darkness
seeing your boyfriend with another girl
standing in the rain without an umbrella
your house burning down
seeing a homeless person and not being able to help him.

Luany Teles, 18

The Saddest Earthquake in My Life

I had an earthquake in my eyes
When I saw my father die
In front of me.

I had an earthquake in my ears
When I heard my father before he died
When he said, "Anwar,
take care of yourself. I love you."

I had an earthquake in my body
When my father hugged me before he died
And I saw him fall down from my hands.

I had an earthquake in tears
When my mouth shouted,
"Dad, don't die. I need you."
When my ears heard and the people cried.

When my dad died in front of me
My tears flowed over from my eyes.
That was the real earthquake.

Kaid "Anwar" Alameri, 16

A Long Time

An earthquake in my heart
The weather was cold or hot, I didn't want to know
And my name, I didn't want to remember

I will stay here for a long time
Morning to night, I will miss you
When I was drunk, I could see you
In the dream, I could approach you forever.

Chun Him Ip, 16

Slashed in Two

I am an immigrant in America.
Slashes are in my body.
Immigration tears me apart.
Half of me is left in China.
In my dreams, I am walking in my hometown.
In the days, I am studying in my school.

William Huang, 18

Blonde and Perfect

Blonde and Perfect
she glitters in the sun
in the shiny pink perfect dress
perfect pink lipstick on her lips
appears in thin air, in her bubble
her sparkly wand, good she is
Glinda the good witch.

Laughter in the air
laughter everywhere
every turn I make
there it is, laughter oh laughter.

The path of darkness
mysterious and creepy
laughter oh laughter
creatures lurk deep in the dark.

A wave of hatred
flows in the air
a wave of fear
lurks over the sky
like a blanket of fog
the fear paralyzing everyone.
Laughter oh laughter
then a wave of sadness
rushing through everyone's blood.
A wave of pain
sinks into everyone's heart
stabbing feelings in every inch
of everyone's body.

Ariana Montemayor, 12

Car Lights in a Dark Garage

Poetry should stick to you
Like molasses or peanut butter
Poetry should bounce around your head
Like a 25-cent rubber ball
Poetry should grip you for the longest time
Like a vise lightened by an ox
Poetry should illuminate areas
Of your brain you never go
Like car lights in a dark garage
Poetry should be easy
Like thoughts leaving
Someone who can talk.

Hilsen Zhang, 17

The Wind

I am the wind
that blows your window curtains
apart, the wind that blows the leaves
off the trees and onto the dry grass.

I am that wind!

I can be gentle
or mad, but no matter what,
I am still that wind.
When I am gentle, I blow
not even an ant,

but when I'm mad, I shatter everything.

I am the wind!

I can mix
with water
to become hurricane
and after, nothing but rain.
I am the rain
going away
as the summer comes.

But I'll be back.
I will be born from rivers, lakes, and oceans.
I am that rain.

Anthony Mejia, 13

My First Busted Lip

My tongue swirls around a strip of bleeding flesh
My first busted lip
The vein beats silently between my fingers
Blue, red, white, distended in the mirror
Bleeding lips, licking at the wounds
Speaking with no one to talk to
Everything is stiff, still, pouring with pain
My tongue gets used to the taste.

Celia La Luz, 17

Dead Man Walking

I don't think about Tubman
or think about slavery,
but my presence is known.
There's no limit to bravery.
I'm not a bully
but I'm fully
equipped with the metal.
So if you drain my gas tank
then I'm pushing the pedal.
I'm a fighter not a lover
steady missing my brother.
It's like I'm already dead
without the casket and cover.

Diante J., 17

The First

What I remember about that day
is it was raining heavily
and tears rained down my cheeks
and our four luggage bags lay quietly in the taxi
and it was silent in my foyer
and I went into the taxi
and the door closed
and my aunt let off firecrackers to see us off
and I looked out through the wet window
and I felt it was a very beautiful city

Same old furnishings about the quiet room
Nothing about the emptied family

Yanqing Yang, 17

Two Rooms Filled with a Gang of Thoughts...My Mind

I live in a doorway
Between two rooms
A room on how it is
And a room on how it was

I hear fresh blood
Spraying the streets
As hard as glass hitting the kitchen floor
Gunshots
Pop! Pop!
Mothers crying
Brothers dying
Police trying...
(Who were actually there three hours late)
They made it just in time
To see me bury my feelings towards the world
How I feel about
Families putting blood on their doors
As a sign of protection

I peek in the other room
My mom out of the hospital
Giving birth to me
She was in so much pain
Yet she's so happy
As I peek at myself crying
I'm wondering
What was I thinking when I was that age?
Why can't I think that way now?

Brandon Franklin, 17

Getting Ready

Today I feel an earthquake in my head
like a level ten earthquake
some building ready to fall down
When the earthquake ends
I feel quiet
like the sea and oceans in winter time, nobody at sea
I'm an egg getting ready to hatch
from a nest
A baby fish ready to swim
A sun shining so bright
So special in the night

Chun Him Ip, 16

poor old rotting flower
there is nothing to do with
you but to compost

Ivan Cheng, 9

Your Heart

Your heart should shine,
your heart is a gold mine.
You're the only one
who can dig through it.
There's a very large pit
to your deepest, darkest secret.

Lena Zheng, 10

Shock 5
the eye that sees at night

Adolescence

The house had no walls.

The walls were glass
you could see through.

Every time you jumped
the glass would shake
from the vibration of your jump.

There was a thunderstorm.

Some of the glass shattered
but the house did not
fall apart, never.

Monique Chanduvi, 14

Necklace

My necklace hangs in my heart.
It is love but also death.
It is the eye that sees at night.

When the necklace breaks,
my heart breaks with it.

The black necklace,
necklace of the crow.
The crow
wears the necklace on its neck.

The necklace is hanging
from the headboard of my bed
and accompanies me in the morning.

The necklace is outside the window
looking at my face,
hanging in my heart,
the necklace of fear and love,
hanging over a flower,
a flower inside my heart.

Necklace the color black
like love.

Alicia Ortega, 15

What World Are We Living In?

When I think too much the planet becomes a question
   mark.
But I know the rich always win.
The dreams I always wanted become a goal
but the anger got to me and became a reality.
The anger is feared by so many
my feeling is hard to explain.
It's like looking in the mirror and looking for your soul.
There is so much hate in a planet we try to save.
When reality hits it hits us with love
in a crazy underwater way.

Ricardo O., 18

Heart...and Knives

Those knives caused a lot of people's deaths,
especially my best friend's.
I was playing soccer with him inside the yard of my house.
There were a lot of knives above the fence.
We had fun together.
Nothing could disturb our enjoyment.
Suddenly the ball went over the fence.
My best friend climbed the tree.
He wanted to jump over the fence to get the ball.
When he was on top of the tree he fell down
and the knives went inside his heart.
The blood came out from his heart.
The blood was dark and red, immaculate.
I looked at his face.
I saw his smile like innocence.
If you look closely at the knives
you will see tracks of blood on top.
The knives feel upset about what they did
and they want to kill themselves
but how, they don't know.
If you can hear the knives
you will hear them cry
and talk with themselves:

"Why did we kill that heart?"
"Why did we kill that heart?"
You know why?
Because his heart was affectionate.
His heart was clear like the rain
falling from the sky.
His heart was also extensive like the ocean.
I can't forget my best friend
and what happened to his heart.
His heart lives in my memory.
So I always go to the fence
near the knives
and talk with them like crazy.
I can hear what the knives say
and what they feel.

Kaid "Anwar" Alameri, 16

Entering the Heart

Sadness is red
because it enters
into the heart.

It looks like a drop
of life.

It feels like a lump
in the throat.

Jonathan Lopez, 16

Justice

When I was walking towards my house
this guy ran up to me and snatched my purse.
I ran after him till I caught him and told him to leave
   me alone,
and that girl that I didn't like came and called the
   authorities.
I asked why she helped me, and she told me it's called
   justice
and you need to stand up for what is right.

Andriaj Cirklelis, 10

Earth, No Sun

The breeze of your voice
calmed my earth within.
Beams of your sun
helped me grow with no end.

But when it rained
your sun was covered
with an ugly gray cloud,
the breeze became a strong wind
blowing everything down.

When the rain stopped
my earth was left wet,
cold, and lonely

and still I wait for a sun to hold me.

Jeremiah M., 20

An Obstacle

Between me and you
a rock interrupts our way.
Our obstacle is hard
and difficult to pass.

Between me and you
we have an abyss to cross.
We don't even have a bridge.
I will build one to cross it.

Between me and you
the door itself
makes no promises.
It is only a door.

Franklin Bracamonte, 17

Getting Out of Bedrock

A tsunami of thoughts
stress me out
thinkin' of the street life
and going a new route.

People wreck my thoughts
and get me off track,
but Unc's magnitude of knowledge
puts me ahead of where I was at.

I hit bedrock from memories
of people dead,
but I force myself to move
ahead.

To have a one track mind
is hard, and I'm going to keep on
trying, even if it feels
like I'm dying.

Live a new life,
reject the fame of the street.
Give the next generation
knowledge to be free.

Jamal S., 18

Nothing Till You've Fallen

People said I was stubborn.
Often told me I was hardheaded,
good for nothing,
shit for brains,
and a menace to society.

      I thank those people,
those people who put me where I am today.

I am like a plum tree, if it's not snowing
I'm not beautiful.
      I am getting into
trouble and getting locked up
so I can grow.
I grow at the same speed as a bamboo tree.
I am similar to the bonsai tree.
I grow big and strong in rough areas.
I am grateful for a troubled life.
You don't gain anything until you have fallen.
I am
I am
I am
I am Tree
I will live for
hundreds of years, strong, beautiful
and tall.
I am.

Hardy H., 17

At Least with Me

Sunday, April 4th, 2004
My father arrived
In the visiting room
At 850 Bryant Pod D
He let me know
All of his children
Were in jail
Me
My little brother
And older brother
This was real
Messed up
My father was more hurt
Than I was
I could look in his eyes
I could see this
Even though he never let the words
Out of his mouth
I promised him
That he would never
Have to go
Through this again
At least with me.

Wakima Clark, 20

Compatriot

Many of us dream with open eyes
the precious and priceless moment of coming back to
   our home.
I have seen people breathing hope through their noses
holding in their lungs
an intense desire to smell once again
the aroma of the soil where they were born.
Unfortunately they have to let their breath out
and with it their dream dissolves in the air.
I dream of my home country
the beauty of the forest
with the singing of the birds in the morning
and the light sun through my window
on a hot day of summer.
I miss the big yellow bowl
shining harshly over my head
the blue heaven painted in white
with the funny shapes of the clouds.

Jorge Aburto, 17

As I Walk

As I walk I follow my soul
in the black, arranged world.
I have strength, hope and dreams
to follow my lead.

Elisa Batis, 17

This Is the Year

This is the year that my friends won't die.
They will last as long as the trees
reach towards the sky.
There will be no guns or bullets
to shoot people in the head.
The pills you OD on will turn into M&Ms
And the cars will disappear so no one will crash.
This will be the year I will remember the lost,
I will remember the past.
This is the year the sun will rise.
There will be no hurt
No deadly surprise.
Life is like a box of chocolates
Or so I've heard.
This is the year I'll soar like a bird.
The thunderous silence won't pound in my head.
This will be the year I'll love the life I live.

Michelle Vail, 16

Sunset

My heart cracks
like a knife.

When a tree is alive
it shines like the sun.

When the sun goes down
it looks like a rose
opening.

Shahil Patel, 10

A Free Place

Poetry should travel around the world
and visit different cultures and say hi to them.
Poetry should go to Iraq
and come back and tell the world about it.
Poetry should destroy the border line and
make the world a free place.
Poetry should be a doctor or a scientist
and find the cure for AIDS.
Poetry should travel to the future
and come back.
Poetry should tell us what's wrong with the world
and help us fix it.
Poetry should make sure the world won't
come to an end.
Poetry should be blue like the sea
and have millions of lives in it.
Poetry should make sure the world is safe.
Poetry should help me finish this poem.
Poetry should stop time
and not commit a crime
and that is what poetry should do.

Nestor Cerda, 13

Dark Figure

I am that tall dark figure
Who stands
Under the city's night light
Staring at the buildings
Which scrape the sky
Waiting for the day
I will reach that sky
And hear the sounds of the city
From my empires
For now I read the thoughts of those
Who have succeeded
Before me
I fear that my name
Will not be remembered
But I do not cry
For myself
I am far too busy
With others
Their pain
They give to me
Expecting me
To obliterate it

Brandon Kissinger, 17

Anger & Poetry

Anger is like breaking
all the plates
and ripping out
the windows.

Poetry is like seeing
the whole world.

Alma Garcia, 12

Through Time

I am the women in the fields bringing
the cotton and the corn to yield,
going to sleep, hands bleeding and my
back has whelps with the design of a tree.

I am the seed of the free.

I am the young female slave who
was raped and impregnated
by my master.

Walk with me
through the year 1955
when Rosa didn't get up on
her feet and out of her seat for some
white man.

I am the seed of the free.

Let me take you back when all people
wanted was equality and peace,
when people were protesting against
Jim Crow laws.

I am the seed of the free.

Now come back to the future with me
and watch who and what I become.
I am a young black man selling what
I've got to sell to support my family because
I am too qualified or not qualified enough
for a job of minimum wage.

I am the seed of the free.

I am the proud father hanging my son's
college diploma on my wall.

I am the black nurse checking a man's
blood pressure in a nurse's office.

I am the seed of the free.

I grow up between the cracks of the sidewalk.

I sprout up walls like a spider.
I creep into your room.

My vines wrap around you like a bear hug.

My thorns cut you to prove that I am strong
and dominant.

My roots walk the streets
and my leaves cover the world to take over
with strength and power.

I am the seed of the free.

We will rise and blossom like the daisies
in the spring.

Like the orchids in your backyard
we will rise over the fences.

You can rise from that dark corner
you're hiding in.

We will rise across the nation
and our beauty will grow
and our voices will be heard.

I am the seed of the free.

I am the voice of all people everywhere.
Clink! Clink! I come to you from the railroads
that my people built with our callused hands
because no one would take the job.

I am the seed of the free.

I am the Mexican who crossed the border
for a new life but was denied and pushed back.
I kept crossing until I was welcomed with open arms.

I am the seed of the free,
I am the seed of the millennium,
the country, the universe,
of the world's accomplishments.

Being the seed of the free
doesn't just begin with me,
it begins with you.

We
    are the seed
                of the free!

Marie Antoinette Osborne, 15

Andrew

for my brother

Her middle is swollen
A globe that will one day crack
And release an American.

Her belly is a planet
That has noisy earthquakes;
The rumbles whisper a name:
Andrew.

Instead of on her shoulders
She carries the earth in her womb.

Now I embrace not one,
But two worlds.
One maternal
And young,
The other genderless
And without a birthday.

After emerging from the egg
Big, dark eyes are revealed.
Their twin reflections
Hold a hint
Of happiness
Enveloped in fresh tears.

When I am older,
He asks me how I know his name
Before he existed.
When he is younger,
I tell him because he told me.

Monica Sanchez, 16

Human Target

I will use my hands to disperse
the darkness in the sky
I want to see the whole
moon.

Francisco, 16

After 6
i carry my home in my heart

Making New Things Before Us

As the world turns I walk on it.
Before the sun moves we're out there
Covered with light
Discovering new things with the world around us
Every day.
Forgiving people for the bad things they've done.
God's city is covered with candles and light.
Horror dragons digging holes down, down to the ground.
Igloos frozen like an ice cube floating on water.
Jaguars running faster than ever, with
Kangaroos hopping around.
Lions roaring louder than ever before as we're
Making new things before us.
Never before seen a golden apple dropping into someone's
    mouth.

Nadessa Corea-Levy, 9

Venus: A Love Poem

All the trees bleed in winter
all the branches grow thick
the sea turns cold
the streets ache with silence
and one star
that's really a planet
shines so bright
in this dark
      dark
      night.

Adrian Mowbray, 16

The Letter O

a girl is crying and you can see her bellybutton
we are living on the earth
my friend's eyes

Sobia Khan, 16

Who Doesn't See Beauty in Pain?

She wears a parted smile
Drunk with the promise of today
Sober with the truth of tomorrow
Who doesn't see beauty in pain?

I want to lift every voice when I scream
Does the dry earth smile when God weeps?
Are kids excited when Daddy steals their toys for a fix?
Do you think the man who sells drugs to a pregnant woman
Doesn't strut when he wears his new outfit?
You don't see beauty in pain?

Some people are prisoners of circumstance
Stuck in a world small as the palm of your hand
It's hard to maintain
When the pressure of the next meal
Is putting weight on your brain
Hunger gives a baritone moan

It's eight o'clock in the morning
She had an argument 4 breakfast
Off 2 work she goes

Where do I find happiness?
I looked for it in love, a pet and in that black fist
My Grandma seems to think it's just me
I guess she doesn't see
Her son's problem with drinking
I want to lift every voice when I scream
Make a symphony with my growling stomach

I shook pain, turned it upside down,
Looking for strength and beauty
Amidst scars, tears, and defeat
Finally I lifted every voice when I screamed

Martrice Candler, 19

Inside

You walk inside myself and it is winter on a dark night.
Not summer nor fields of wildflowers.
It is a huge field of rolling winds.
You follow the sound of emptiness
And you climb a stairway of mystery and curiosity
Made of just pure thoughts.
You are in my emptiness.
You have your peace.
The loneliness is a privilege.

Mikael La Torre, 16

Lost Girl

There was
a girl that
was lost in
the city.
She was
so scared she
ran from
people. One
day she
recognized
a street
name. She
knocked on
the door.
A woman
opened the
door. The
woman started
to cry and
hug the girl.
It was the
girl's mother.
The lost girl was a found girl.

Cheyenne Tores, 9

Sisters

Strong bond true life twins
Love hate brawl stay kin
Talk hear yell close ears
Still love does not dim

Noelle Turcotte, 17

My Mom Is Everything

Her depth is the blue of the sky
and the ocean.
She is posole
steaming up from the Monday night
table.
She is an eagle that protects
her family from danger.
She is an earthquake
when she gets mad.

My mom is a park where people
run and play.
She is an ocean
where the fishes swim everywhere.
She is the cake people like to eat.

My mom is an Aztec princess
where she admires her people
from the pyramids of Mexico.
She is a spring season
that makes the people become happy.

She is a beautiful flower
in a cold winter,
the church where people feel safe.

My mom is a Saturday
that I want to never come to an end.
She is a lake at the edge
of the desert, the heart of my life!
She is everything for me,
the motivation to continue living
in this world.

Ruben Hernandez, 15

Below Yellow Glass

I am making a house
for my wife and me.

I am making a house with windows
of yellow glass.
Looking outside there is light and hope.

There is a nice place
for our children
to play games in the garden
and listen to their mother
tell a story. The children's
voices are quiet and peaceful.

There is laughter coming
from the floor,
the luck of children,
the health of my mother and grandmother,
and my own strength.

Jin Wei Deng, 17

The Sun and My Life

The sun is beautiful,
it is like the blaze
of hot glaze on a donut.

The sweetness
just like the sun.

When it rains
the sun is always there.

When it is cloudy
it is there too.

It's like family,
they are always there.
The sun is too.

When people pass away,
I look up to the sun
and see them smiling.
That tells me
that they are happy
so I am happy
and I can't get happier.

I love the sun.
It feels like
looking at
a thousand worlds.

Cocatli Martinez-Alvarado, 10

Kobritika

The color Kobritika shines in the shadows of burned animals,
lying on the trees of the Amazon of Brazil.
The color Kobritika is the laziness that stops time
from moving at a fast pace.

Kobritika makes you happy every time
you write a poem to your best friend.
Kobritika flies over the rivers, over the mountains,
over the oceans, over the waterfalls,
over California, over all around the world.

Kobritika is the taste that stays in your mouth
after drinking a sugary coffee at your house.

Kobritika is the feeling of being happy,
of being sad, of being angry, of being mad.
Kobritika is loving hate while a knife
goes through your lungs affecting your life.

Kobritika goes down with the sun to
sleep and plan a future for the children
who don't have food nor a home.

Kobritika is the pain of seeing so much
death, when the war never stops.
Kobritika is the belief in God. It is the way
you pray. It is the God who is always caring
and watching you. It is the feeling of accomplishment
for something good.

Kobritika is water burning your hands
while janitors are working hard cleaning
offices, houses, even their own, trying
to do their duty, their chores.

Kobritika is the memories of learning how to ride
a bike when you are small.

Kobritika is the bite of a cobra that killed
a ten year old child in India,
on a trip to the jungle.

Kobritika makes you suffer, makes you cry.
Kobritika is the reason you're still alive.

Valentina Prado, 16

Compassion

I am Saturday of every week
which makes people happy and relaxed.
Like the glasses I help
the people who have myopia.

My real name is Market Street
with many stores
to make people's lives colorful.

As the sunshine
I bring brightness to the earth.
I am an ocean
covering 75% of the world.

Call me the red of everyone's heart.

My real name is a dog
to accompany every lonely person.

As the winter of the year
I make the world white and neat.
Call me an ice cream
to make people feel cool
during the hot summer.

Like the grasses
I embellish the whole forest.
I am the whole of the world.

Heki Zhao, 16

Ode to Hopscotch

Hopscotch.
It's waiting for me at Bessie School.
I play it every day.
The lines are almost gone.
The people that play are very good.
Watch not to step on the lines!
When I throw my key
it flies through the air
without touching the lines.
When I do a bunnyhop
it feels like I'm diving
into the water.
It feels like I'm hopping
in the parade.
Yesterday when I did cross
it felt like
I was a gymnastics performer
showing my friends
what I can do.
When I play hopscotch,
ten is my home.

Lily Nguyen, 9

Family

Family is like
the harbor
where ships can take a rest.

Jialie Liu, 16

Moon Craters

What is in the moon craters in the black as raven night?
What you think is wrong and what I think is right.
Why does the moon shine? There's only one reason—
just because the fairies dance throughout the seasons.
It's fairy dust that makes it glow
in the craters so low.
So the next time you see the moon's craters,
think about its tiny, sparkling invaders.

Maya Castleman, 12

Tranquility

Poetry should make people laugh all day,
Let a little joy into people's lives,
Bring peace and "Let Freedom Ring!"

Poetry should smell like French fries straight off the oven,
Sweet yet forbidding,
The scented aroma whiffing through the room,
As fragrant as flowers.

Poetry should make people cry,
Break down and let go,
Emotions on overdrive and let loose
The pain, anger, passion, and joy.

Poetry should look like the stars,
Twinkling in the sky,
The age-old question with no beauty to compare to,
Lovelier than peace, while at the same time,
More hideous than death.

Poetry should feel like water,
Slipping through my fingers like the Sands of Time,
Slipping, slipping,
Out of my grasp and gone forever
'Til the world is once again renaissance.

Poetry should be warm like a soft yellow, crackling fire,
No hate, no fear, tranquil, powerful,
Mightier than a mountain, frail like a rock.

Poetry should be hope,
Within the reach of a person's mind.

Suzanne Ly, 13

Night Lights

I see water.
I see cars going
over the bridge.
When it's dark
in the night
I see lights
on the bridge
and I dream
I'm in the middle.

Araceli Navarrete, 6

The Fourth of July

My heart should be a Roman candle.
Convicts celebrate the Fourth
with T-bone steak
and all the watermelon you can eat.
The irony is bitter
but the melon is sweet,
and though it might be a proud gesture
to refuse the food,
I have more hunger than pride.
So I sit alone
with a slice of melon in my hands,
watching staff
like they watch me.

I ate my heart
to stay alive.
I carved it like meat
and salted it with tears.

I don't care about the calendar.
Whatever day I leave here
will be my Fourth of July.

Like the rest of me
my heart is stubborn.
It tastes like melon on my tongue
and fills my mouth with seeds
and fills my head with seeds
and fills my empty chest with seeds
and I will toil in sorrow,
spitting out my soul like seeds
until my heart grows whole again.

John E. Sweeney, 17

Reflection

The reflection of my future,
standing in the water
with a cross behind me:
the lines of challenge,
light
of my goals
and dark
of my problems.

Rhea Lyn Ferrer, 14

Nothing at All

Some days I'm the hot fudge sundae
served at McDonald's.
Other days I'm the refried red beans
served in a ceramic plate.
Yesterday I was nothing at all.

I carry my home in my heart as
I travel around the world.
I am no citizen or resident
of this or that country
cuz nationality and frontiers were invented by some loner
some political and philosophical talker.

The city where I was born means mass of water
and in my blood there's water.
So I carry my city in my veins
whether my path heads south, central, or north.
I represent the mixed cultures of Spanish conquistadors
Indian warriors and American Modernism.
My home is my mom's medical point of view
and my father's religious belief.
My home is my grandmother's manzanilla tea.

Some days my brown skin makes me stand out as beautiful.
Other days it is the cause of my oppression.
But in any way I'm proud of it.
Proud of my accent and Latin background.

It's funny how some days I'm a wetback
for my American reality.
And other days I'm a gringa
for my Nicaraguan reality.
But other days I'm just myself
living in a galaxy far away from here.

So my home is a box that holds
my past, my present and wonders about my future.
It's my lasting moment of happiness and forgiveness.

Luz Aburto, 16

Between Me and the World...

Between me and the world
You are a flower, a future
A field covered with smells
You are red, yellow
A night that keeps the stars company

Between me and the world
You are a mountain, a painting
A field very high with bushes
You are blue, yellow
A night that is black

Between me and the world
You are a little song
of things that you would do
of things that you would say

Between me and the world
you are a future, a world
For all people need a good future
Sweet sweet memory of the world

Truong An Do, 17

Let the Rain Kiss

Let the rain kiss
people who sell drugs
so they stop selling drugs
to the teenagers.

Let the rain kiss
every weapon
so they can't kill
people anymore.

Let the rain kiss
beggars so they have food
and someplace to live.

Let the rain kiss
the old people
so everybody will respect them.

Let the rain kiss
all countries
so they will grow peace
in their hearts.

Let the rain kiss
the illiterates
so they can read and write.

Let the rain kiss
me
so I can pray for them.

Edson So, 17

Once upon a Time

Once upon a time
There was a lake
And water turned
Big or small
Because he was in a bad mood.
One day a woman came
And she knew the water
Was in a bad mood.
So she went back to her house.
Then she came back
With a pair of shoes
And she said loudly,
"Take the shoes!"
And the lake took them.
And the water took them.
And the water was happy again.
Then she went
Into her house
And looked into her closet
For one more pair of shoes.

Egbert Gonzales, 8

Poetry Bottle

When I was eleven a wise old woman
in my dream gave me her poetry bottle.
She would come into my dreams often,
but then mysteriously disappear.
I don't know how I got the bottle or why.
All I know is that I had it inside of me.
The poetry bottle would stay closed up tight
with a silver cork.
It would stay quiet and never make a sound.
When it was totally silent
with paper in front of me,
the silver cork would pop open.
Slowly, silver smoke would drip out,
creating a blanket of clouds that would cover me.
It seemed to cover me with my past childhood
I had forgotten. My hands would move
very quickly, and when I opened my eyes
words would appear on my paper.
Beautiful poems would slip out of the bottle.

I have been secretly using my poetry bottle
for six years now.
Every year the silver smoke gets thicker and thicker.

It will continue getting thicker
until the blanket suffocates me from the inside.
And then I will turn into silver smoke
and be wrapped in the bottle forever.
And the bottle will once again be refilled
with the silver cork closing it tight,
until one day, someone else opens it.

Asefa Subedar, 17

House without a Door

The sun is the hope to recuperate
all that was lost,
the mirror that illuminates
our happiness to live.

The sun is the light I need
to think and create.
The sun lights my way
so I can walk straight.

The sun is the eye
of every person in the world.
The sun is a house without a door
that everyone can enter.

Dennis Villalta, 17

Nana Don't Die

My grandma gave me 2 dollars 4 lunch money
Why she did that?
I can't eat
Thousand pound boulder burdens my back
A dollar on a bammer sack
A dollar on beedies
Blindsiding myself

I see a face in every window
We all high and drunk
If it's seasoned and crispy
We all gone eat.

I got to beat the fiend in me
My reality
My addiction to the beedies and weed
And my slave mentality.

Looking in the wrong direction
I listened for the sun
And let the night consume me

II.

Police brutality
The slave masters in disguise
Hungry to see another black motherfucka die
We both hungry but
I'm praying to survive
He's praying to dominate
Our lives collide

On the dolla bill it says in god we trust
But they hide behind they white skin
Give ya guns, drugs and
A slave master's street to claim
Miseducate ya
Date-rape ya
Coke you up
Then penitentiary
I mean, penetrate ya.

Look in the subliminal message
In only god u should trust

III.

You act like I make these blocks on the corners
I was given these blocks on the corner
My niggaz is wolves and they roll 'n' pack
They didn't make them gunz
They was given that

IV.

My hunger pain isn't the only one in the world
I hear all the hungry bellies cry
I hear all women throwing their wings away
I hear the pain in every prayer being whispered
Just to eat and be safe and hear the wind blow one more
    time
I hear every cheek crinkle when ghetto kids smile
Man they face was frozen in hardship
I hear every crack with that ice break
Nana don't die

V.

In my last life I was a scientist
With death from disease all around me
I was striving on a hunt for a cure
In the midst I fell in love with the mystery.

Disease conquered.

I was reincarnated an At-Risk Youth
With nowhere to go and everything to lose

They want us to forget about the royalty in our blood
Let my soul tell it all
Truth will be how God judges me
Nana don't die

VI.

I'm transparent
Whether you see this love or pain
Whether you see the hunger
I'm transparent
Nana don't die—the truth just set me free.

Martrice Candler, 19

Put me somewhere else
where it is dark and there is no sun,
so I can be bright
and see how well I shine.

Sandro Haro, 9

About the Editor

Judith Tannenbaum, who currently serves as training coordinator for San Francisco's WritersCorps program, has been poet-in-residence in many community settings, from primary schools to maximum security prisons. Her books include the memoir *Disguised as a Poem: My Years Teaching Poetry at San Quentin* (Northeastern University Press/University Press of New England, 2000), *Teeth, Wiggly as Earthquakes: Writing Poetry in the Primary Grades* (Stenhouse Publishers, 2000), and many small books of poems. Judith also edited, with Valerie Chow Bush, WritersCorps' *Jump Write In! Creative Writing Exercises for Diverse Communities, Grades 6-12* (Jossey-Bass, 2005).

WritersCorps History

Since its inception in 1994, WritersCorps has helped more than 40,000 people in some of the United States' most economically disadvantaged neighborhoods improve their literacy and self-sufficiency. WritersCorps has transformed the lives of thousands of youth at risk by teaching creative writing, giving voice to young people whose voices have been systematically ignored or disregarded. With its award-winning publications and highly regarded reading series, WritersCorps has become a national arts and literacy model.

WritersCorps was born out of discussions between Jane Alexander, former Chair of the National Endowment for the Arts (NEA), and Eli Siegel, then-director of AmeriCorps. Today, hundreds of writers have committed to teach in their communities, inspire youth, and work diligently to create a safe place for young people to write, and to discover themselves in the process. WritersCorps teachers make lasting connections with their communities and become valued mentors and role models.

San Francisco, Washington, DC, and Bronx, NY, were selected as the three initial sites for WritersCorps, cities chosen for their exemplary art agencies with deep community roots and their traditions of community activism among writers. In these three cities, WritersCorps' established writers, working at public schools and social service organizations, have helped people of virtually every race, ethnicity, and age improve literacy and communication skills, while offering creative expression as an alternative to violence, alcohol, and drug abuse.

In 1997, WritersCorps transitioned from a federally funded program to an independent alliance, supported by a collaboration of public and private partners. DC WritersCorps, Inc. is now a nonprofit organization while the San Francisco and Bronx WritersCorps are projects of the San Francisco Arts Commission and Bronx Council for the Arts, respectively. WritersCorps has developed a national structure administered by the three sites to provide greater cooperation and visibility, while at the same time allowing each site the independence to respond most effectively to its communities.

To learn more about WritersCorps contact:

Bronx WritersCorps
718-409-1265
www.bronxarts.org/gp_bwcorps.asp

DC WritersCorps
202-332-2848
www.dcwriterscorps.org

San Francisco WritersCorps
415-252-4655
www.writerscorps-sf.org

Aunt Lute Books is a women's press that has been committed to publishing high quality, culturally diverse literature since 1982. In 1990, the Aunt Lute Foundation was formed as a non-profit corporation to publish and distribute books that reflect the complex truths of women's lives, and to present voices that are under-represented in mainstream publishing. We seek work that explores the specificities of the very different histories from which we come, and the possibilities for personal and social change.

Please contact us if you would like a free catalog of our books or if you wish to be on our mailing list for news of future titles. You may buy books from our website, by phoning in a credit card order, or by mailing a check with the catalog order form.

Aunt Lute Books
P.O. Box 410687
San Francisco, CA 94141
415.826.1300
www.auntlute.com
books@auntlute.com

This book would not have been possible without the kind contributions of the Aunt Lute Founding Friends:

Anonymous Donor   Diana Harris
Anonymous Donor   Phoebe Robins Hunter
Rusty Barcelo   Diane Mosbacher, M.D., Ph.D.
Marian Bremer   Sara Paretsky
Marta Drury   William Preston, Jr.
Diane Goldstein   Elise Rymer Turner